Coffee Art

coffeeschool.com.au

Thanks

Paula Benmayor for your love, support and ideas.

coffeeschool.com.au
113 Arundel St Glebe
NSW 2037 Australia
Phone: 02 9552 6771

Published by Daniel Benmayor 2004

First printed 2004

Cover photo coffee beans Paris Spellson

ISBN 0-646-43189-7

Contents

Coffees

Espresso Short Black	30ml coffee served in a small cup.
Long Black	Half a cup of hot water in a regular cup followed by 30ml coffee.
Caffè Latte	1/3 coffee. 2/3 milk and a little foam served in glass.
Flat White	1/3 coffee. 2/3 milk and a little foam served in regular cup.
Cappuccino	1/3 coffee. 2/3 milk and a lot of foam. Chocolate on top served in a regular cup.
Macchiato	Espresso with foam.
Piccolo Latte	Espresso with milk and foam served in small glass.
Hot Chocolate	Chocolate with hot milk served in a tall handled glass.
Mocha Coffee	30ml coffee with hot chocolate served in a tall handled glass.
Vienna Coffee	Long black with whipped cream and chocolate on top.
Iced Coffee	1 scoop ice cream. 1/3 cold coffee. 2/3 cold milk. Whipped cream and chocolate on top. Served in a tall glass.
Iced Chocolate	Coat glass with chocolate syrup. 1 scoop ice cream. Cold milk, whipped cream and chocolate on top. Served in a tall glass.

Group handles & filters

Single Spout Group Handle

Use for one regular or one weak coffee.

Single Filter

Holds 8 grams of coffee.

Double Spout Group Handle

Use for two regular, two weak or one strong coffee.

Double Filter

Holds 16 grams of coffee.

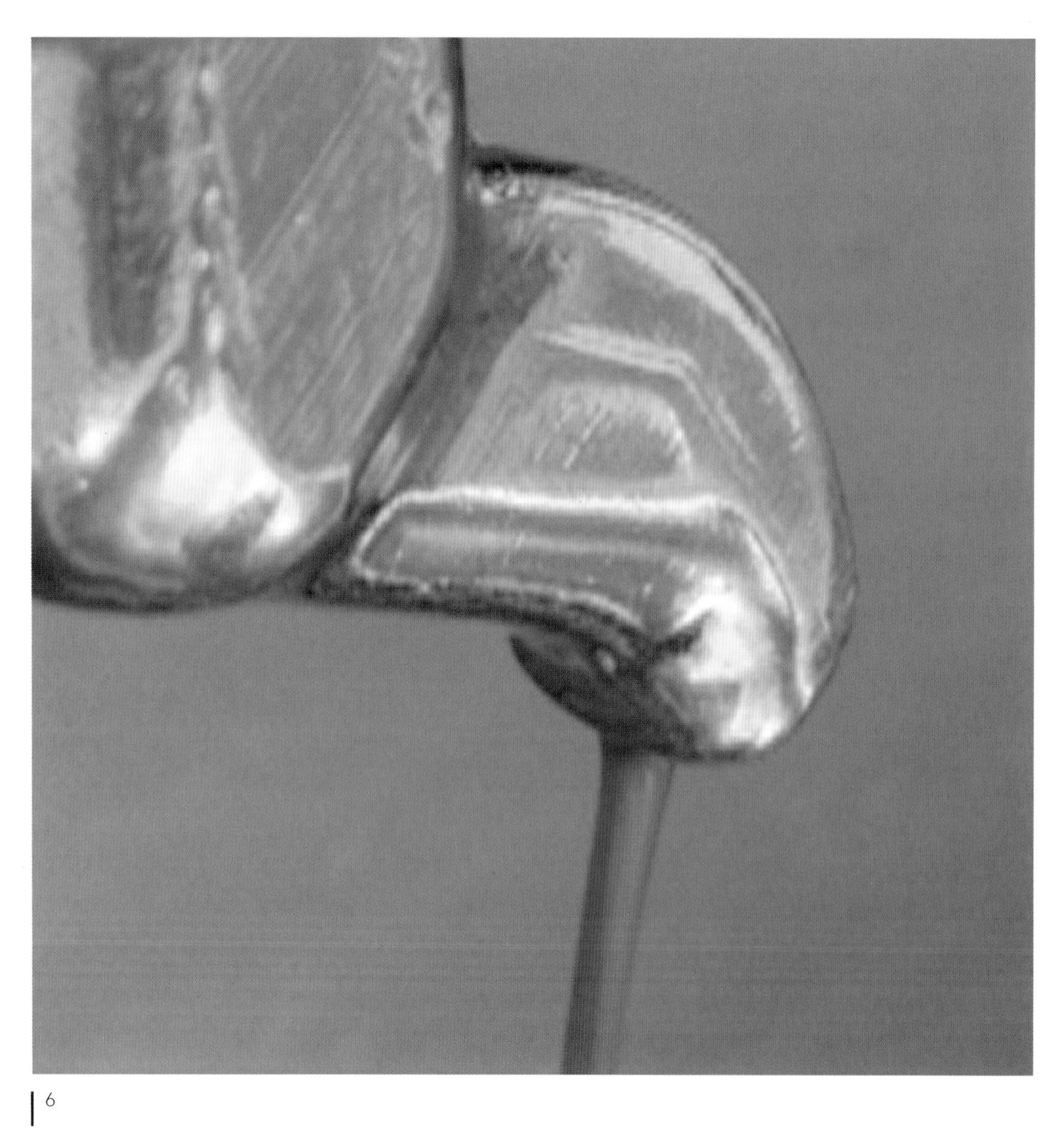

Crema, Grind & Extraction

The grind of the coffee determines how fast the coffee is extracted. Ideally the coffee should pour like honey leaving a thick layer of Crema on the top. The Crema is the caffeine or richness of the coffee and should always be present if the coffee is freshly ground to the correct size.

If the coffee extracts very quickly and there is very little Crema the grind is too coarse. Conversely if the coffee extracts very slowly and drips rather than pours from the spout, it is too fine.

Barista – Coffee Artist

The Barista is the espresso machine operator. The Art of Barista begins with the preparation of the 'shot' of coffee which is 30ml. Regularly the milk follows and the coffee is completed. The Barista's ability to develop a relationship with each customer is paramount. This relationship is formed by greeting each customer with a smile that says:

'I am here to prepare your coffee the way you like it.'

Identifying each customer by name as well as remembering their preferred coffee will definitely create a genuine coffee experience.

To be a fast and efficient Barista always follow the three steps:

1 Bang Bang

2 Rinse Wipe

3 Pack / Tamp

While the coffee is extracting from the espresso machine, foam your milk and place a saucer and a teaspoon.

Bang Bang

Knock the coffee out of the group handle.

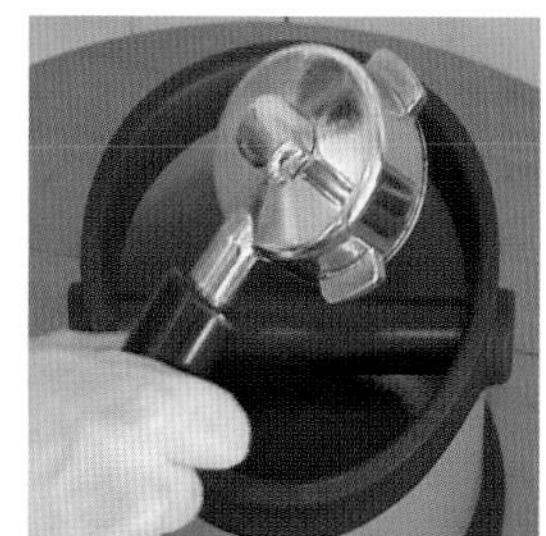

Rinse Wipe

Rinse and wipe the group head and handle removing old coffee grinds.

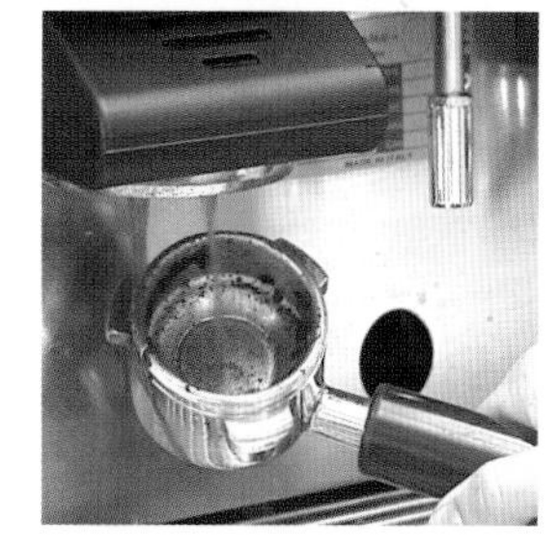

Pack/Tamp

Pack the coffee gently into the filter of the group handle. Never 'choke' the coffee by pressing too hard on the tamper.

Milk Temperature

The correct milk temperature is always achieved by placing your hand on the side of the milk pot. This method is known as Pot Technique. To determine the correct temperature of the milk, touch the pot and ask yourself the question:

"Can my hand stay there?"

If the answer is NO turn off the steam immediately!

If your hand can no longer tolerate the heat of the pot you have achieved the correct temperature. This method will also ensure you never commit the most common error in coffee, burning the milk. Alternatively a thermometer may be used whereby the milk is heated to 66 - 76 degrees Celsius.

Tips

Use cold milk when foaming as you will have more time to create foam before the milk reaches the correct temperature.

You can re-use heated milk once only providing you add fresh milk first.

Fill the pot with only one third of milk allowing for plenty of space in which to make the foam.

Foaming Milk

Under

Begin by placing the steam arm under the milk in the centre of the pot.

Power

Always give maximum steam pressure.

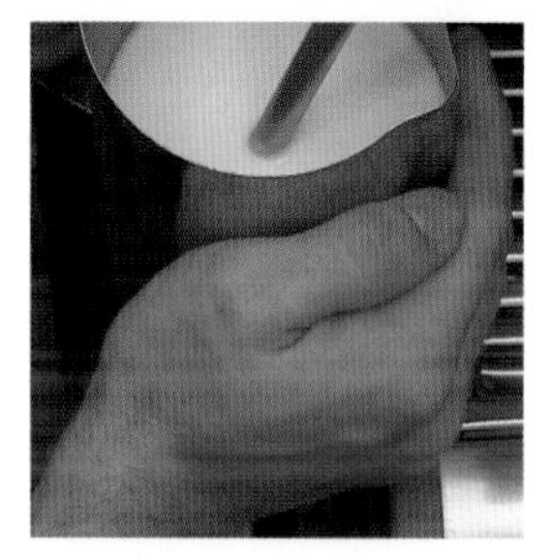

Pot Technique - Touch the pot

Ask yourself "Can my hand stay there?" No. Turn it off!

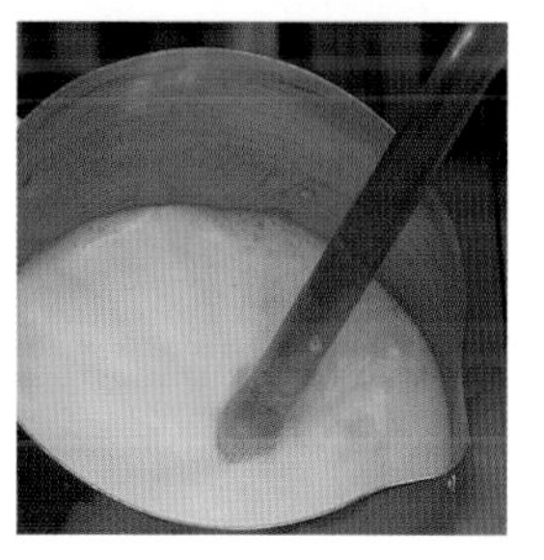

Lower the pot slowly to make foam

Always keep the tip of the steam arm in the centre of the pot just under the surface of the milk as you lower the pot slowly.

Silky Milk

The perfect milk for Coffee Art is smooth in texture with a shiny appearance 'meringue like'.

Lower the pot very slowly not allowing large bubbles to occur.

Finish with approximately one third more volume than what you started with.

Tap the milk jug on the bench firmly to remove any remaining bubbles.

Swirl the jug in a circular motion until a shiny, smooth texture is achieved.

Regular Coffee

Eight grams of coffee packed into the single group handle. Extract the coffee for approximately 20 seconds, which will give 30ml of coffee or one third of the cup. This is the base of every regular strength coffee. It is the same as an 'Espresso' or 'Short Black' and is also known as a 'Shot' of coffee.

Over Extracting

The grind can only be used once. After pouring for around 20 seconds there is no more caffeine left to extract from the grind. Do not pour beyond 30ml. For a Long Black Coffee always add half a cup of clean hot water from the hot water spout to the cup first to avoid over extracting.

Weak Coffee

Extract less coffee into the cup. Approximately 15ml or less depending on how weak you desire. Do not change the amount of coffee packed into the group handle, which remains at 8 grams.

Never re-use the same group handle just because you have extracted less than a regular 'Shot'.

The grind has already been used regardless of how little is extracted.

Strong Coffee

Using the double spout group handle pack 16 grams of coffee. Place the cup under the two spouts and extract a 30ml shot. You will notice a thicker Crema because the coffee is more concentrated. This will also create a darker brown base for Coffee Art.

You are permitted to extract up to 60ml in a strong coffee as you are using 16 grams of coffee. The double spout handle is also used for two regular coffees or two weak coffees.

Cleaning

Blind filter

The Blind filter cannot be seen through as there are no holes, hence its name. It is used only to clean the group heads of the machine. Using a teaspoon remove the normal filter for making coffee and replace it with the Blind filter. All commercial coffee machines will come with a Blind filter. Blind filters should not be used on most domestic coffee machines.

Espresso Machine Chemical Cleaner

Place half a teaspoon of Espresso machine chemical cleaner in the blind filter. Put the handle in the group head and turn it on to allow the water to flow for 5 seconds. Stop the water and leave for 5 seconds. Repeat this process several times. 'Back Wash' the machine thoroughly. Always throw away the first coffee made after using chemical cleaner.

'Back Wash' Cleaning

Place the Blind filter in the group handle. Place the group handle loosely in the group head and turn the water on. Softly jiggle the handle inside the head many times always checking the colour of the water remaining in the Blind filter. If the water remaining in the Blind filter is clean, the group head is clean. This process is called 'Back Washing' or 'Flushing' the group head. It must be done at least once a day or after each kilo of coffee used which is approximately 100 cups. Back washing can be done on domestic machines using the normal filter.

Art Tools

Teaspoon is used to pick up crema and froth to create small circles and draw lines. To create a thinner line, move the teaspoon quickly. For best results always hold the teaspoon vertically. The teaspoon is also used for layering.

Tablespoon is used to hold back froth when pouring. It is also used to pick up froth and create large white circles in the crema.

Skewer is used for drawing lines, patterns and placing small dots. For best results insert skewer vertically at least 2cm.

Small Stainless Steel Jug is used for pouring coffee and chocolate preparation when layering.

Fine Tip Sauce Bottle is used for striping Hot Chocolate glass with chocolate preparation.

Chocolate Preparation

Mix 90% chocolate powder with 10% hot water and stir until smooth.

Place inside fine tip sauce bottle and refrigerate for Hot Chocolate.

Place into a small stainless steel Jug at room temperature for Layered Coffees.

Techniques

Brown Base

The brown base is the canvas on which you will design your Coffee Art. To achieve this canvas, continuously pour the milk slowly in the centre of the glass in the same place at the same speed. If white appears pour directly on top of it until it disappears. To create a darker brown base use the double spout group handle.

Drawing

Use the Skewer to draw lines. Insert it into the crema and drag it through the foam to create the desired pattern. It is also used to pick up foam and crema and place small dots. It is important the Skewer is wiped clean after every use to avoid disfiguring the design.

Layering

Pouring over the back of a teaspoon will slow down the flow of the liquid being poured preventing it from hitting the bottom of the glass.

Chasing Hearts

Slowly pour milk into the centre of the glass to create a brown base.

Using a teaspoon pick up foam and make three dots.

Place skewer deep into crema.

Pull skewer through the centre of each dot in one movement.

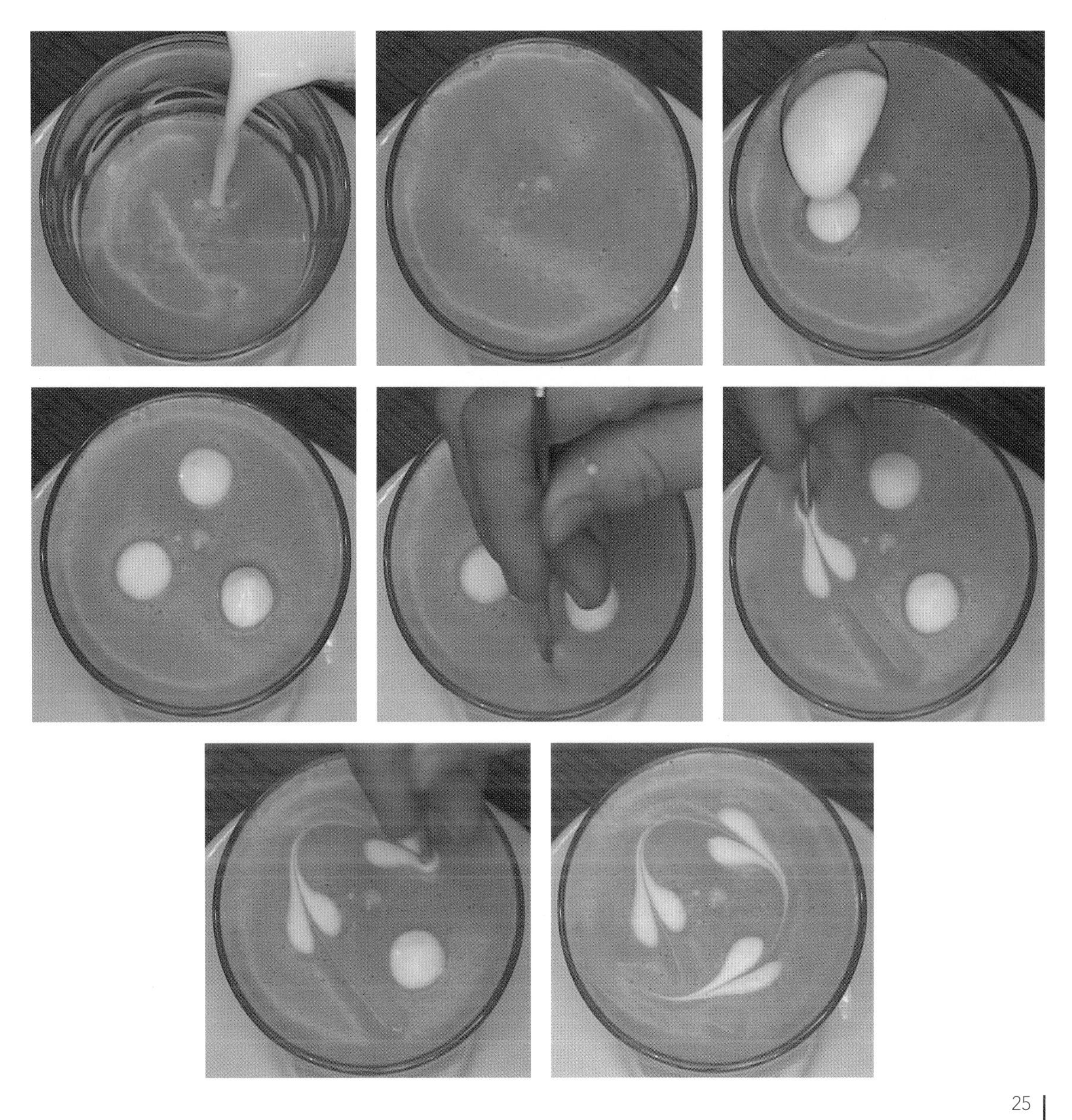

Four Leaf Clover

Create a brown base.

Using a tablespoon pick up foam and make a large circle in the centre of the crema.

Place skewer deep into the crema and pull directly into the centre of the circle and lift out gently.

Repeat at every angle.

Flower

Create Four Leaf Clover.

Split each petal in half again.

Place skewer deep into the centre of foamy petals
and drag through each petal to the rim of the glass.

Repeat with each petal.

Insert a dot of crema directly into the centre of flower.

Flower with hearts

Create Four Leaf Clover.

Using a teaspoon place one small dot of foam between each petal.

Place skewer deep into crema.

Pull skewer through the centre of each dot of foam to create hearts.

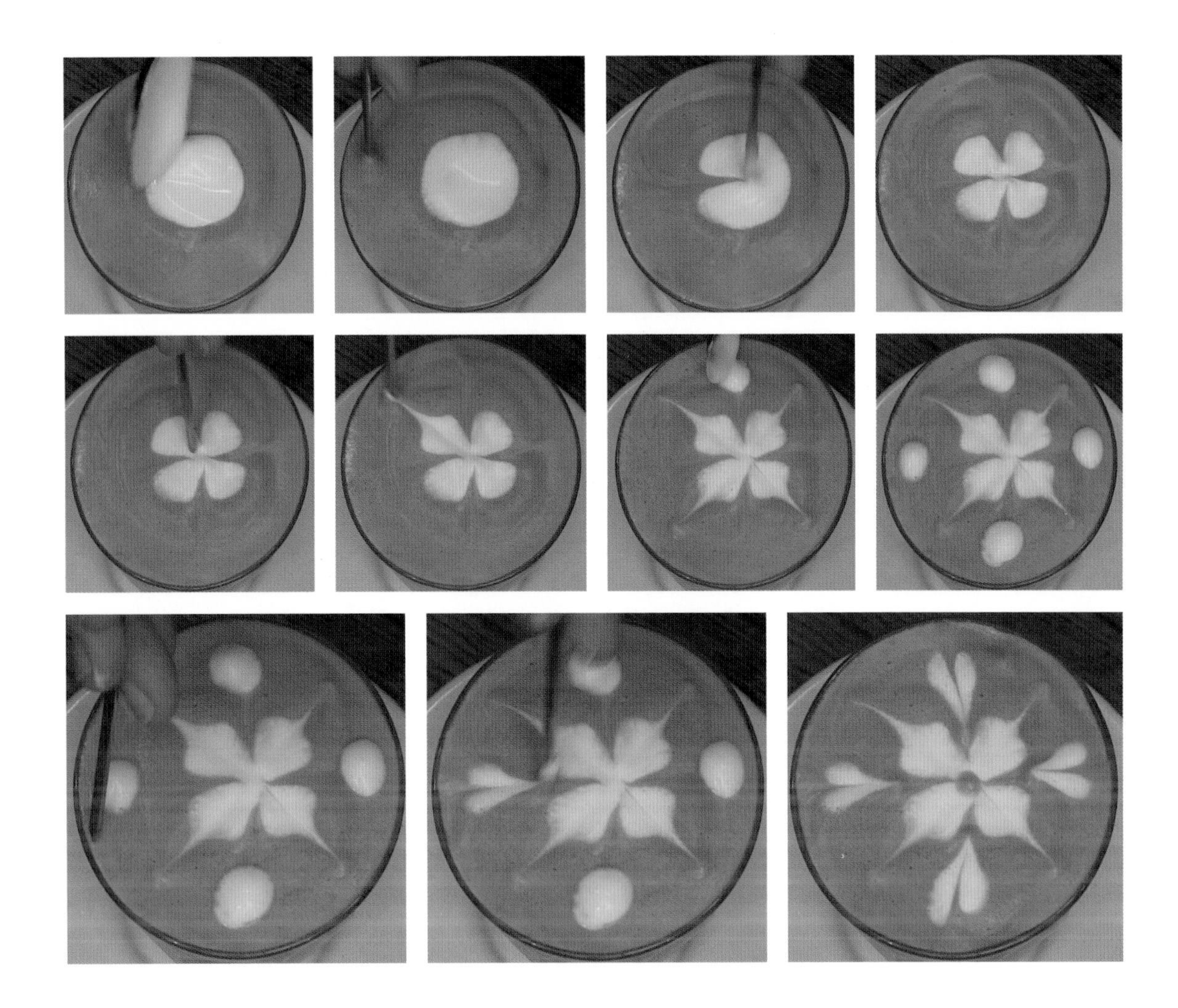

Spiral

Create brown base.

Using a teaspoon place a line of foam through the centre.
To create a thinner line, move the teaspoon quickly.

Place another line of foam to create a cross.

Using a teaspoon place four small dots.

Insert the skewer deep into a dot and drag through each dot before spiralling towards the centre of the glass in one movement.

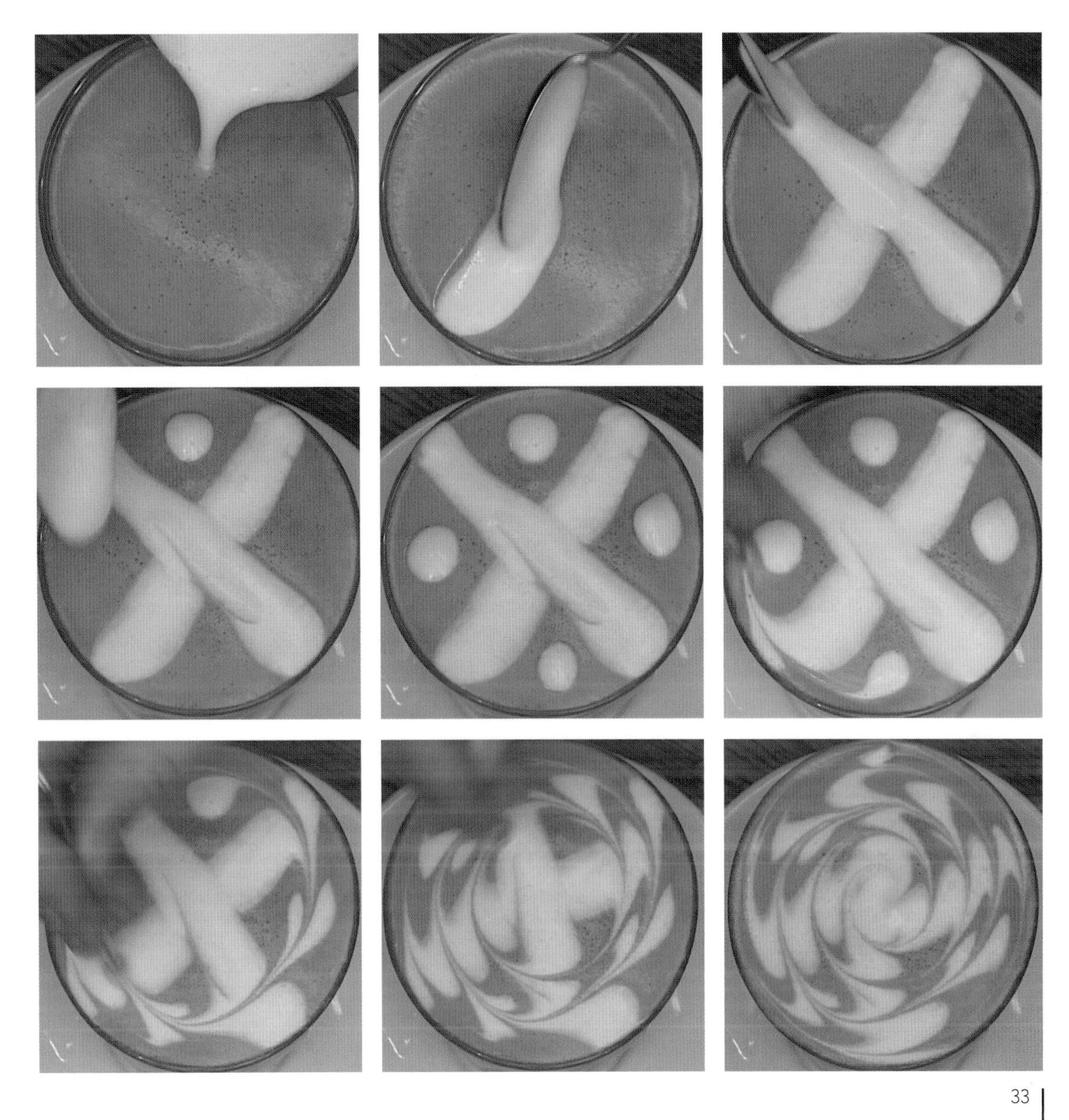

Seagulls

Create a brown base.

Make three parallel lines of foam.

Place a small dot of foam on both sides.

Place skewer deep into a dot.

Following the contour of the glass drag the skewer through to the other dot and repeat in reverse two more times.

Rotate skewer around the rim of the glass several time sto create a border.

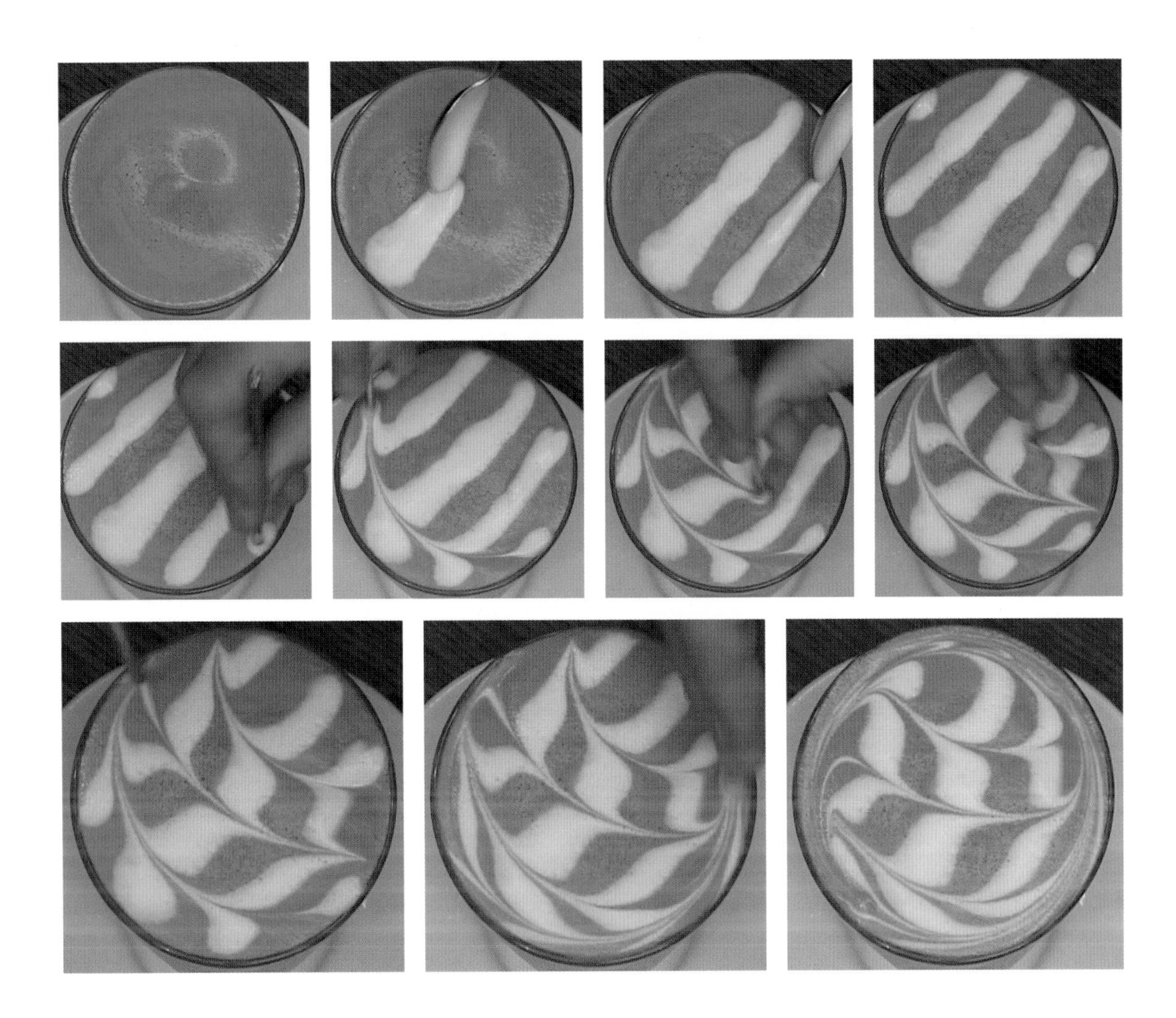

Target Heart

Using a tablespoon place a circle of foam
in the centre of the glass.

Using a teaspoon pick up crema and place directly
into the centre of the white circle.

Using a teaspoon place a smaller dot of foam
inside the crema circle.

Using a skewer pick up crema and place directly
in the centre of the target.

Insert skewer at the edge of the glass and pull through
the centre of the target.

Lips

Create white centred target.

Insert skewer deep into centre of target and pull to one side then repeat pulling skewer to the opposite side.

Spider Web

Repeat lips at other angles.

Flower

Between each web place the skewer into the crema at the edge of the glass and pull towards the centre. Repeat at every angle.

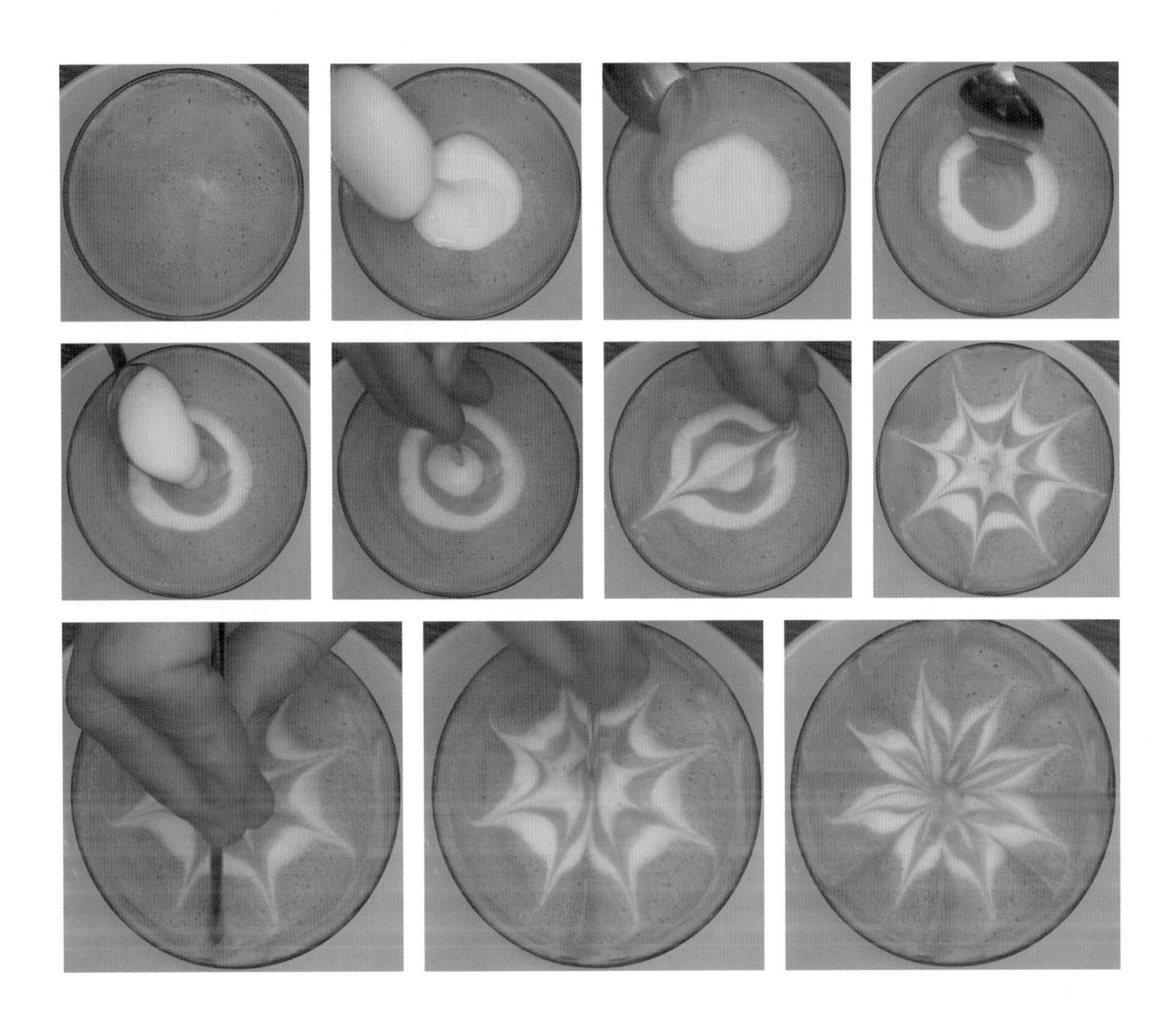

Sunshell

Make a spider web.

Place the skewer at the edge of the glass
and rotate several times.

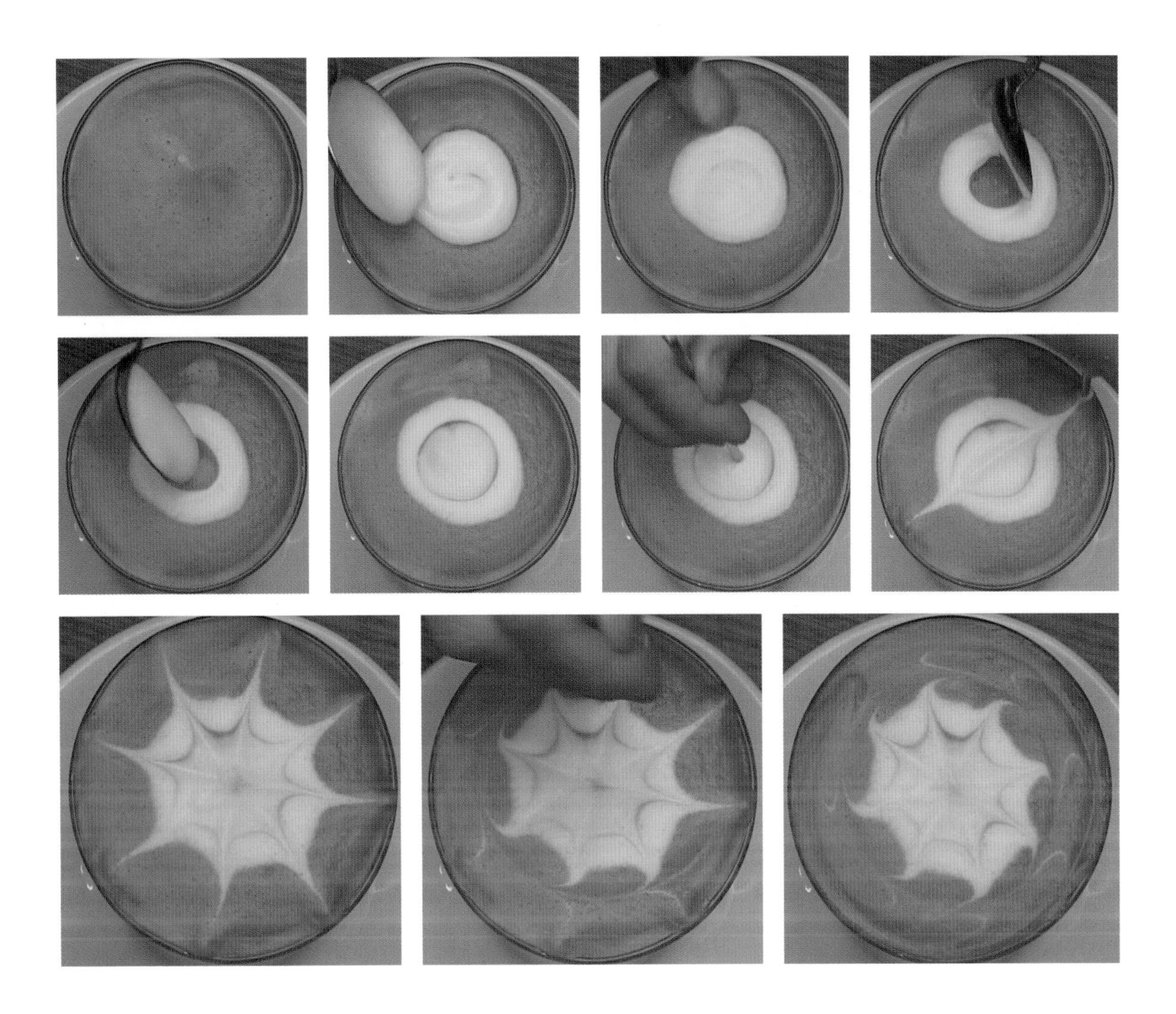

Smiley face

Using a small teaspoon make three dots of foam for the eyes and nose and a line for the mouth.

Place the skewer at the edge of the mouth line and shape the mouth into a smile.

Using a skewer pick up crema to dot the eyes and nostrils.

Pick up more crema and draw a line through the mouth.

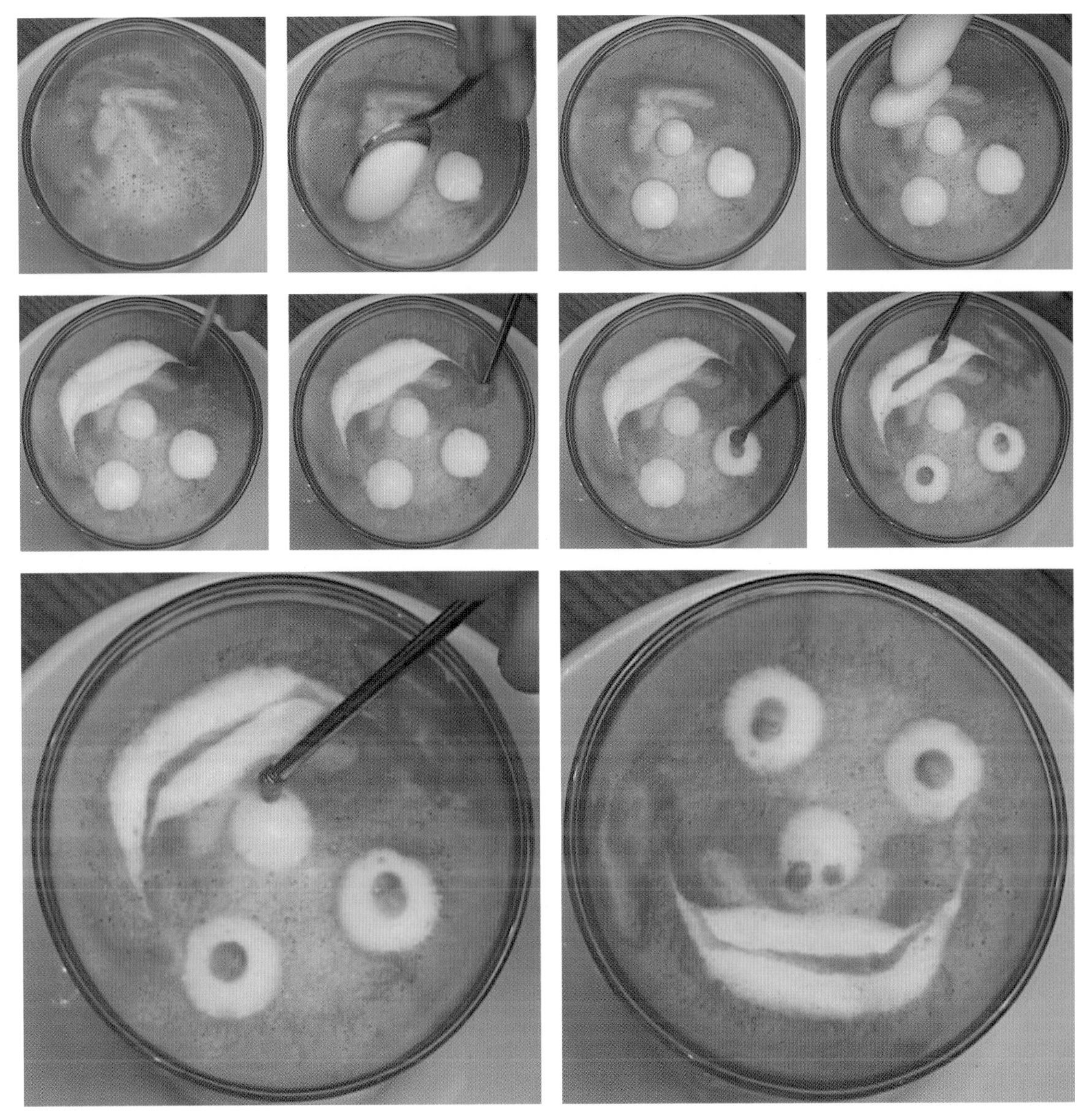

Free pour heart

Pour textured milk at the edge of the cup
creating patterns with the foam.

Pour again on the crema, jiggling the jug quickly from side to side
and a white patch will form on the crema. Increase the speed
of the pour and move the jug forward to create the heart.

Hearts

Make a free pour heart.

Using a teaspoon place two small dots of foam
on either side of the heart.

Place the skewer in the crema and drag it through two
of the dots in one movement. Repeat for the other two dots.

Flat White Sea Gulls

Pour foam into the centre creating a border of crema.

Using a skewer pick up crema and create three parallel lines and a dot on both sides.

Following the contour of the cup drag the skewer through to the other dot and repeat in reverse two more times.

Rotate skewer around the rim of the glass several times to create a border.

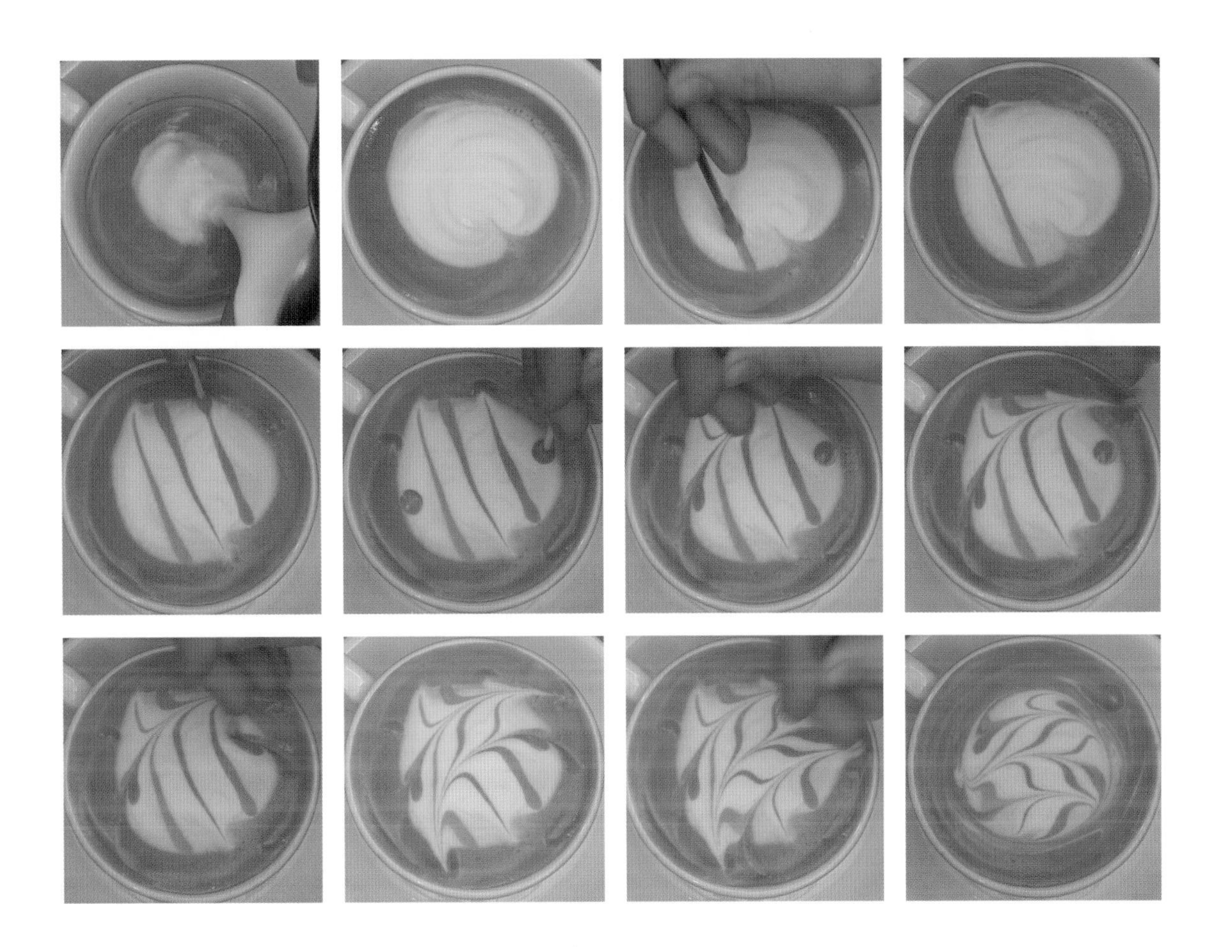

Leaf

Starting in the centre jiggle the pot side to side backward then straight forward.

Insert skewer into the crema and pull backward in a Zig-Zag pattern then forward straight through the centre in one motion.

Flat White Chasing Hearts

Pour foam into the middle of the cup
maintaining a border of crema.

Using a teaspoon pick up crema and make three dots.

Place skewer deep into foam.

Pull skewer through the centre of each dot in one movement.

Layered Piccolo Latte

Extract a shot of coffee into a small glass.

Gently spoon a thick layer of foam.

Slowly pour the milk over the back of a teaspoon
into the centre not allowing it to hit the bottom of the glass.

Layered Caffè Latte

Fill a tall narrow glass to just below the rim with foamy milk.

Slowly pour a shot of hot coffee over the back
of a teaspoon into the centre of the glass.

Leave to settle before serving.

Layered Mocha Latte

Fill a tall narrow glass to just below the rim with foamy milk.

Pour chocolate preparation over the back
of a teaspoon into the centre of the glass slowly.

Pour a hot shot of coffee over the back of a teaspoon
directly into the centre of the glass slowly.

Leave to settle before serving.

Striped Hot Chocolate

Using a fine tipped sauce bottle pour cold chocolate preparation down the side of a tall glass several times to create stripes.

Pour foamed milk into the centre of the glass until full.

Dust with chocolate.

Layered Babycino

Fill a small glass to just below the rim with very foamy warm milk.

Slowly poor chocolate preparation over the back of a teaspoon into the centre of the glass.

Dust with chocolate.